healthy
recipes

DELICIOUS, HEALTHY RECIPES
FROM AROUND THE WORLD

HELEN ADAMS

This is a Parragon Publishing Book
First published in 2004

Parragon Publishing
Queen Street House
4 Queen Street
Bath BA1 1HE, UK

Created and produced by The Bridgewater Book Company Ltd.

ISBN: 1-40543-160-1

Printed in China

NOTE

*This book uses imperial, metric, and US cup measurements. Follow the same units of
measurement throughout; do not mix imperial and metric. All spoon measurements
are level: teaspoons are assumed to be 5 ml and tablespoons are assumed to be 15 ml.
Unless otherwise stated, milk is assumed to be whole, eggs and individual vegetables
such as potatoes are medium, and pepper is freshly ground black pepper.*

*Ovens should be preheated to the specified temperature. If using a fan-assisted oven,
check the manufacturer's instructions for adjusting the time and temperature.*

*Recipes using raw or very lightly cooked eggs should be avoided by infants, the elderly,
pregnant women, convalescents, and anyone suffering from an illness. Pregnant and
breastfeeding women are advised to avoid eating peanuts and peanut products.*

Contents

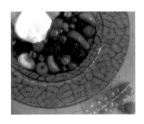

Introduction

Many of us have taken on board the message that what we eat impacts significantly on our health. However, it is easy to become bewildered by the complexities and contradictions in the advice on different foods and dietary regimes that we now face on a daily basis. This book offers a refreshing and inspirational approach to healthy eating based on sound nutritional

principles, and offers a range of easy-to-prepare yet imaginative recipes. The exciting flavors and textures in all these dishes will serve as an antidote to the perceived view that a healthy diet is rather restrictive. This is food that you can really enjoy while improving your health and well-being at the same time.

Healthy Eating Guidelines

In order for your body to maintain good working order, it needs to have a regular and balanced supply of nutrients. This means making the right choice of foods, and nutritionists have developed a way of helping us without having to grapple with detailed nutritional data. They have identified the basic food types and divided them

into five separate groups. These groups are shown here, in descending order of nutritional importance for maintaining a balanced diet.

Breads, Cereals, Pasta,
Noodles, Rice, and Potatoes
These foods are rich in carbohydrates, which provide the body with energy, and are low in fat. They contain B vitamins, selenium, calcium, and iron, as well as fiber. Up to one-third of your daily food intake should be chosen from this group.

Vegetables and Fruits

These nutritious foods are rich in vitamins, particularly A, C, and E, known as antioxidants, and minerals such as calcium, potassium, magnesium, and iron. They are extremely good sources of fiber and are also virtually fat free. You can eat as many as you like of these, and most health organizations recommend eating

at least five portions of vegetables and fruits in total per day.

Meat, Poultry, Fish, Beans, Nuts, Seeds, and Eggs

These foods are our main source of protein, essential for maintaining the body's functions. Meat, poultry, and fish are rich in B vitamins and minerals such as iron, zinc, and magnesium, but they also contain varying amounts of saturated and unsaturated fat.

Milk, Cheese, and Yogurt

Dairy foods offer good sources of calcium, provide protein, and also contain the vitamins A, D, and B_6 (riboflavin). However, they are also high in saturated fats, so your consumption needs to be limited. When buying foods from this group, try to choose lower-fat varieties to help in this way.

Fats and Sugars

These foods are essential to a healthy diet, but they are needed in small quantities only. It is preferable to eat more unsaturated fats than saturated fats. Unsaturated fats are found in olive oil and other vegetable oils, oily fish and fish oils, butter, avocados, nuts, and seeds.

Healthy Ingredients and Options

While carbohydrate-rich foods are the mainstay of a healthy diet, we need to be wary of falling into the trap of eating them with saturated fats and sugars—for instance, breakfast cereals with sugar and milk, pasta with creamy sauces, bread spread with butter and jelly, or potatoes in the form of fries, deep-fried in oil. There are many other ways to enjoy carbohydrates without counteracting their beneficial effects. For extra benefits, opting for whole-wheat or whole-grain varieties of bread, rice, pasta, and breakfast cereals will maximize your intake of dietary fiber and vitamins.

Variety is the key to getting the most from vegetables and fruits in your diet, in terms of both the different nutrients they have and their fiber content, in addition to taste and texture. Bananas, for instance, are rich in potassium, which can help to regulate blood pressure, and citrus fruits are high in fiber and vitamin C.

Spinach, carrots, and bell peppers offer beta-carotene, which the body converts into vitamin A. Some studies have found that lycopene, which gives tomatoes their bright red coloring, can help to reduce the risk of prostate cancer in men, and possibly cervical cancer in women. It appears that canned or other types of processed tomatoes are even more beneficial than the fresh variety.

You can avoid loss of vitamins from vegetables and fruits by taking a few simple steps in their preparation. Avoid peeling them where possible, avoid letting them stand in water before cooking, and avoid overcooking them.

Your choice of protein source has an important part to play in maintaining a healthy diet. Skinless turkey and chicken are relatively low in fat, particularly saturated fats, although the brown meat is fattier than the white. Lean cuts of pork are surprisingly low in fat—more so than beef or lamb. While white fish is low in fat, oily fish, such as salmon, tuna, mackerel, herrings, sardines, and anchovies, contains omega-3 fatty

acids, which are thought to be protective against heart disease and strokes, and may be helpful for those suffering from arthritis. Tofu is a particularly healthy protein source: it is low in saturated fat and cholesterol and contains protective antioxidants. Dried beans, peas, and lentils are another good, lowfat source of protein, but they are best served with whole-grain rice and plant foods to provide the correct balance of nutrients. Nuts are high in fat, but it is mostly of the unsaturated kind which, rather than raising blood cholesterol levels, may even help to reduce them. Hazelnuts, walnuts, and almonds are good choices.

Fatty foods are seductive because the fats and oils they contain are phenomenal flavor-boosters. However, other healthier ingredients can take the place of fats in contributing to the taste of dishes—try using herbs and spices, garlic, fresh gingerroot, tomato paste, olives, capers, reduced-salt soy sauce, Worcestershire sauce, Tabasco sauce, stock, vegetable and fruit juices, and wine.

Healthy Cooking Methods

Once you have chosen the right foods for a healthy, balanced diet, it is vital to follow through with a healthy approach to cooking them. Steaming is a particularly good method that requires no additional fat and retains all the nutrients and flavor, while broiling, grilling, or griddling (using a dry cast-iron or aluminum ridged grill pan on the hob) seals in all the flavor with little or no need for fat. Microwaving is also a fatfree cooking method.

Rapidly stir-frying foods in a preheated wok with a minimal amount of oil is also a relatively healthy cooking method, and again maximizes the taste and texture of ingredients. Using a large, heavy-bottom, nonstick skillet, you can dry-fry fresh lean ground meat or bacon, thereby releasing its own fat, which can then be drained away.

Use a proprietary oil spray for shallow-frying, or alternatively, try sautéeing vegetables without any additional fat in a covered skillet or pan, where they will cook in their own juices.

Soups, Appetizers & Snacks

Tomato &
Red Bell Pepper Soup

Sweet red bell peppers and tangy tomatoes are blended together in a smooth vegetable soup that makes a perfect appetizer or light lunch.

serves 4

2 large red bell peppers

1 large onion, chopped

2 celery stalks, chopped

1 garlic clove, crushed

2½ cups vegetable stock

2 bay leaves

1 lb 12 oz/800 g canned plum tomatoes

salt and pepper

2 scallions, finely shredded, to garnish

crusty bread, to serve

Method

❶ Preheat the broiler to hot. Halve and seed the bell peppers, then arrange them on the broiler rack and cook, turning occasionally, for 8–10 minutes, or until softened and charred.

❷ Let cool slightly, then peel off the charred skin. Reserving a small piece for the garnish, chop the bell pepper flesh and place in a large pan.

❸ Mix in the onion, celery, and garlic. Add the stock and bay leaves. Bring to a boil, then cover and simmer for 15 minutes. Remove the pan from the heat.

❹ Stir in the tomatoes and transfer to a food processor or blender. Process until smooth, then return to the pan.

❺ Season to taste with salt and pepper and heat for 3–4 minutes, or until piping hot. Ladle into warmed bowls and garnish with the reserved bell pepper cut into strips and the shredded scallion floating on the top. Serve with crusty bread.

Cook's tip

If you prefer a coarser, more robust soup, lightly mash the tomatoes with a wooden spoon and omit the blending process in Step 4.

Nutritional Information

Calories	52	Sugars	9g
Protein	3g	Fat	0.4g
Carbohydrate	10g	Saturates	0g

Lentil & Ham Soup

This is a good hearty soup, based on a stock made from a ham knuckle, with plenty of vegetables and red lentils to thicken it and add flavor.

serves 4

scant 1 cup red lentils

6¼ cups stock or water

2 onions, chopped

1 garlic clove, crushed

2 large carrots, chopped

1 lean ham knuckle or 6 oz/175 g lean bacon, chopped

4 large tomatoes, peeled and chopped

2 fresh or dried bay leaves

salt and pepper

9 oz/250 g potatoes, chopped

1 tbsp white wine vinegar

¼ tsp ground allspice

chopped scallions or chopped fresh parsley, to garnish

Method

❶ Place the lentils and stock in a large pan and let soak for 1–2 hours.

❷ Add the onions, garlic, carrots, ham knuckle, tomatoes, and bay leaves and season to taste. Bring the mixture to a boil, then cover and and let simmer for 1 hour, or until the lentils are tender, stirring occasionally to prevent the lentils sticking to the bottom of the pan.

❸ Add the potatoes and continue to simmer for 20 minutes, or until the potatoes and ham knuckle are tender.

❹ Discard the bay leaves. Remove the knuckle and chop 4½ oz/125 g of the meat and reserve. If liked, press half the soup through a strainer or process in a food processor or blender until smooth. Return to the pan with the rest of the soup.

❺ Taste and adjust the seasoning if necessary, and add the vinegar and allspice and the reserved chopped ham. Simmer gently for an additional 5–10 minutes. Garnish with scallions and serve.

Nutritional Information

Calories 219

Protein. 17g

Carbohydrate 33g

Sugars 4g

Fat. 3g

Saturates 1g

Beef & Vegetable Soup

This comforting broth is perfect for a cold day and is just as delicious made
with lean lamb or pork fillet.

serves 4

⅓ cup pearl barley, soaked overnight	1 leek, shredded
5 cups beef stock	1 onion, chopped
1 tsp dried mixed herbs	2 celery stalks, sliced
8 oz/225 g lean rump or sirloin steak,	salt and pepper
trimmed and cut into strips	2 tbsp chopped fresh parsley, to garnish
1 large carrot, diced	crusty bread, to serve

Method

❶ Place the pearl barley in a large, heavy-bottom pan. Pour the stock over and add the mixed herbs, then bring to a boil. Reduce the heat, then cover and simmer gently over low heat for 10 minutes.

❷ Skim away any scum that has risen to the top of the stock with a flat spoon. Add the steak, carrot, leek, onion, and celery to the pan. Return to a boil, then cover and let simmer for 1 hour, or until the barley, meat, and vegetables are just tender.

❸ Skim away any remaining scum that has risen to the top of the soup with a flat ladle. Blot the surface with paper towels to remove any fat. Season to taste with salt and pepper.

❹ Ladle the soup into warmed soup bowls and sprinkle with chopped parsley. Serve piping hot with crusty bread.

Cook's tip

A delicious vegetarian version can be made by omitting the steak and beef stock and using vegetable stock instead. Just before serving, stir in 6 oz/175 g firm tofu, drained and diced.

Nutritional Information

Calories	138	Sugars	2g
Protein	13g	Fat	3g
Carbohydrate	15g	Saturates	1g

Yogurt & Spinach Soup

**Whole young spinach leaves add vibrant color to this unusual soup.
Serve with hot, crusty bread for a nutritious light meal.**

serves 4

2½ cups chicken stock

salt and pepper

4 tbsp long-grain rice, rinsed and drained

4 tbsp water

1 tbsp cornstarch

2½ cups lowfat plain yogurt

3 egg yolks, lightly beaten

juice of 1 lemon

12 oz/350 g young spinach leaves,
washed and drained

fresh crusty bread, to serve

Method

❶ Pour the stock into a large pan, then season to taste with salt and pepper and bring to a boil. Add the rice and simmer for 10 minutes, or until barely cooked. Remove the pan from the heat.

❷ Mix the water and cornstarch together until smooth. Pour the yogurt into a second pan and stir in the cornstarch mixture. Set the pan over low heat and bring to a boil, stirring with a wooden spoon in one direction only. This will stabilize the yogurt and prevent it separating or curdling on contact with the hot stock. When the yogurt has reached boiling point, stand the pan on a heat diffuser and simmer gently for 10 minutes.

Remove the pan from the heat and let cool slightly before stirring in the beaten egg yolks.

❸ Pour the yogurt mixture into the stock, then stir in the lemon juice and stir to blend thoroughly. Keep the soup warm, but do not let it boil.

❹ Blanch the spinach leaves in a large pan of salted boiling water for 2–3 minutes, or until they begin to soften but have not wilted. Tip the spinach into a colander and drain well, then stir it into the soup. Warm through, then taste and adjust the seasoning if necessary. Serve in warmed soup bowls with crusty bread.

Nutritional Information

Calories	227	Sugars	13g
Protein	14g	Fat	7g
Carbohydrate	29g	Saturates	2g

Minted Onion Bhajis

Besan (also known as gram flour) is a fine yellow flour made from chickpeas and is available from supermarkets and Asian food stores.

makes 12

scant 1 cup besan

1/4 tsp cayenne pepper

1/4–1/2 tsp ground coriander

1/4–1/2 tsp ground cumin

1 tbsp chopped fresh mint

salt and pepper

4 tbsp strained plain yogurt

generous 1/4 cup cold water

1 large onion, cut into fourths and thinly sliced

vegetable oil, for frying

fresh mint sprigs, to garnish

Method

❶ Place the besan in a bowl, then add the cayenne, coriander, cumin, and mint and season to taste with salt and pepper. Stir in the yogurt, water, and sliced onion and mix well.

❷ Fill a large, deep skillet one-third full of oil and heat until very hot. Carefully drop heaped spoonfuls of the mixture, a few at a time, into the hot oil and use 2 forks to neaten the mixture into rough ball shapes.

❸ Cook the bhajis until golden brown and cooked through, turning frequently.

❹ Drain the bhajis thoroughly on paper towels and keep them warm while cooking the remainder in the same way.

❺ Arrange the bhajis on a large serving plate and garnish with fresh mint sprigs. Serve hot or warm.

Cook's tip

Besan is excellent for making batter and is used in India in place of flour. It can be made from ground split peas as well as chickpeas.

Nutritional Information

Calories	251	Sugars	7g
Protein	7g	Fat	8g
Carbohydrate	39g	Saturates	1g

Chicken & Almond Rissoles

Cooked potatoes and chicken are combined to make tasty nutty rissoles which are served with stir-fried vegetables.

serves 4

4 oz/115 g parboiled potatoes, grated

1 carrot, grated

1 cup ground cooked chicken

1 garlic clove, crushed

½ tsp dried tarragon or thyme

pinch of ground allspice

or coriander

salt and pepper

1 egg yolk or ½ egg, beaten

2 tbsp slivered almonds, finely chopped

butter, for greasing

lime wedges, to garnish

Stir-fried vegetables

1 tbsp groundnut oil

1 celery stalk, thinly sliced diagonally

2 scallions, thinly sliced diagonally

8 baby corn cobs

scant ½ cup snow peas or sugar snap peas

2 tsp balsamic vinegar

Method

❶ Preheat the oven to 400°F/200°C. Mix the potatoes, carrot, and chicken with the garlic, herbs, and spices and season. Add the egg and bind the ingredients together. Divide the mixture in half and shape into "sausages." Spread the almonds on a plate and coat each rissole in the nuts. Place the rissoles in a greased ovenproof dish and cook in the preheated oven for 20 minutes, or until browned.

❷ To stir-fry the vegetables, heat the oil in a skillet. Add the celery and scallions and cook over high heat for 1–2 minutes, then add the corn cobs and snow peas and cook for an additional 2–3 minutes. Add the vinegar.

❸ Transfer the rissoles and stir-fried vegetables to individual serving plates and garnish with lime wedges. Serve.

Nutritional Information

Calories	161	Sugars	3g
Protein	12g	Fat	9g
Carbohydrate	8g	Saturates	1g

Sweet & Sour Drumsticks

Chicken drumsticks are marinated to impart a tangy, sweet and sour flavor and a shiny glaze.

serves 4

8 chicken drumsticks

4 tbsp red wine vinegar

2 tbsp tomato paste

2 tbsp soy sauce

2 tbsp clear honey

1 tbsp Worcestershire sauce

1 garlic clove, crushed

good pinch of cayenne pepper

fresh parsley sprigs, to garnish

crisp salad, to serve

Method

❶ Skin the chicken drumsticks, if desired, and slash 2–3 times with a sharp knife. Arrange the drumsticks in a single layer in a shallow, nonmetallic container.

❷ Mix the vinegar, tomato paste, soy sauce, honey, Worcestershire sauce, garlic, and cayenne together in a small bowl and pour over the chicken drumsticks. Cover and let marinate in the refrigerator for 1 hour.

❸ Preheat the grill to medium. Cook the drumsticks over the hot coals for 20 minutes, brushing with the marinade and turning during cooking, until the chicken is tender and the juices run clear when a skewer is inserted into the thickest part of the meat. Garnish with parsley sprigs and serve with a crisp salad.

Cook's tip

For an extra tangy flavor, add the juice of 1 lime to the marinade. While the drumsticks are cooking, check regularly to ensure that they are not burning.

Nutritional Information

Calories	171	Sugars	9g
Protein	23g	Fat	5g
Carbohydrate	10g	Saturates	1g

Bruschetta

Traditionally, this Italian savory is enriched with olive oil. Here, sun-dried tomatoes
are a good substitute, and only a little oil is used.

serves 4

1 cup dry-pack sun-dried tomatoes

1¼ cups boiling water

14-inch/35-cm long Granary or
whole-wheat French baguette

1 large garlic clove, halved

scant ¼ cup black olives in brine, pitted,
drained, and cut into fourths

2 tsp olive oil

salt and pepper

2 tbsp chopped fresh basil

scant ½ cup grated lowfat
mozzarella cheese

fresh basil leaves, to garnish

Method

❶ Place the sun-dried tomatoes in
a heatproof bowl and pour over the
boiling water.

❷ Let stand for 30 minutes so that the
tomatoes soften. Drain well and pat dry
with paper towels. Slice into thin strips
and reserve.

❸ Preheat the broiler. Trim and discard the
ends from the bread and cut into 12 slices.
Arrange on a broiler rack and cook under
the hot broiler for 1–2 minutes on each
side, or until lightly golden.

❹ Rub both sides of each piece of bread
with the cut sides of the garlic. Top with
the strips of sun-dried tomato and olives.
Brush lightly with oil and season well with
salt and pepper. Sprinkle with the basil
and mozzarella cheese and return to the
grill for 1–2 minutes, or until the cheese
is bubbling and melted.

❺ Transfer to a warmed serving plate and
garnish with fresh basil leaves. Serve.

Nutritional Information

Calories	178	Sugars	2g
Protein	8g	Fat	6g
Carbohydrate	24g	Saturates	2g

Cheese & Chive Biscuits

These snack-time classics have been given a healthy twist by the use of lowfat soft cheese and reduced-fat Cheddar cheese.

makes 10

1½ cups self-rising flour, plus extra for dusting

1 tsp powdered mustard

½ tsp cayenne pepper

½ tsp salt

scant ½ cup lowfat soft cheese with added herbs

2 tbsp snipped fresh chives, plus extra to garnish

scant skim milk, plus extra for brushing

½ cup grated reduced-fat sharp Cheddar cheese, grated

lowfat soft cheese, to serve

Method

❶ Preheat the oven to 400°F/200°C. Sift the flour, mustard, cayenne, and salt into a large bowl. Add the soft cheese and mix together until well incorporated. Stir in the chives.

❷ Make a well in the center of the ingredients and gradually stir in the milk until the mixture forms a soft dough.

❸ Turn the dough out onto a floured counter and knead lightly. Roll out until ¾ inch/2 cm thick and use a 2-inch/5-cm plain pastry cutter to stamp out as many circles as you can. Transfer the circles to a baking sheet.

❹ Re-knead the dough trimmings together and roll out again. Stamp out more circles—you should be able to make 10 biscuits in total.

❺ Brush the biscuits with milk and sprinkle with the grated cheese. Bake in the preheated oven for 15–20 minutes, or until risen and golden. Transfer the biscuits to a wire rack to cool.

❻ Serve the biscuits warm with lowfat soft cheese, garnished with chives.

Nutritional Information

Calories	297	Sugars	7g
Protein	13g	Fat	3g
Carbohydrate	49g	Saturates	4g

Potatoes with a Spicy Filling

The filling has the Middle Eastern flavors of chickpeas, cumin, and coriander.

serves 4

4 large baking potatoes	**Salad**
1 tbsp vegetable oil (optional)	2 tomatoes, chopped
salt and pepper	½ cucumber, sliced
15½ oz/430 g canned chickpeas, drained	½ red onion, thinly sliced
1 tsp ground coriander	
1 tsp ground cumin	
4 tbsp chopped cilantro	
⅔ cup lowfat plain yogurt	

Method

❶ Preheat the oven to 400°F/200°C. Scrub the potatoes and pat them dry with paper towels. Prick them all over with a fork and brush with oil, if using, then season to taste with salt and pepper. Place them on a large baking sheet and bake in the oven for 1–1¼ hours, or until cooked through. Let cool for 10 minutes.

❷ Place the chickpeas in a large bowl and mash. Stir in the ground coriander, cumin, and half the chopped cilantro, then cover and reserve.

❸ Halve the potatoes and scoop the flesh into a bowl, keeping the shells intact. Mash the flesh until smooth and gently mix into the chickpea mixture with the yogurt. Season to taste. Place the shells on a baking sheet and fill with the potato mixture. Return the potatoes to the oven and bake for 10–15 minutes, or until thoroughly heated through.

❹ Toss all the salad ingredients together. Sprinkle the potatoes with the remaining cilantro and serve with the salad.

Nutritional Information

Calories	335	Sugars	7g
Protein	15g	Fat	7g
Carbohydrate	57g	Saturates	1g

Rice & Tuna Bell Peppers

Broiled mixed sweet bell peppers are filled with tender tuna, corn, nutty brown
and wild rice, and grated reduced-fat Cheddar cheese.

serves 4

generous ¼ cup wild rice

generous ¼ cup brown rice

4 bell peppers, halved and seeded

7 oz/200 g canned tuna in brine, drained
and flaked

11½ oz/325 g canned corn
kernels, drained

scant 1 cup grated reduced-fat sharp
Cheddar cheese

1 bunch fresh basil leaves, shredded

salt and pepper

2 tbsp dry white bread crumbs

1 tbsp freshly grated Parmesan cheese

fresh basil leaves, to garnish

crisp salad greens, to serve

Method

❶ Place the wild rice and brown rice in separate pans and pour over enough boiling water to cover, then bring to a boil. Cook for 40–50 minutes, or according to the package directions, until tender. Drain the rice well.

❷ Meanwhile, preheat the broiler to medium. Arrange the bell peppers on the broiler rack, cut side down. Broil for 5 minutes, then turn the bell peppers over and cook for an additional 4–5 minutes.

❸ Place the cooked wild and brown rice in a large bowl and mix together. Add the flaked tuna and drained corn and gently fold in the grated cheese. Stir the basil leaves into the rice mixture and season to taste with salt and pepper.

❹ Divide the tuna and rice mixture into 8 equal portions. Pile a portion into each cooked bell pepper half. Mix the bread crumbs and Parmesan cheese together and sprinkle over each bell pepper.

❺ Return the bell peppers to the broiler for 4–5 minutes, or until hot and golden brown. Serve immediately, garnished with basil and accompanied with salad greens.

Nutritional Information

Calories	332	Sugars	13g
Protein	27g	Fat	8g
Carbohydrate	42g	Saturates	4g

Red Snapper &
Coconut Loaf

**This fish and coconut loaf is ideal to take along on picnics because
it can be served cold as well as hot.**

serves 4-6

2½ cups coconut liquid (see Step 1)

8 oz/225 g red snapper fillets, skinned

2 tomatoes, seeded and finely chopped

2 green bell peppers, finely chopped

1 onion, finely chopped

1 fresh red chile, finely chopped

scant 3 cups bread crumbs

salt and pepper

butter, for greasing

Hot pepper sauce

½ cup tomato ketchup

1 tsp West Indian hot pepper sauce

¼ tsp hot mustard

To garnish

lemon twists

fresh chervil sprigs

Method

❶ Preheat the oven to 400°F/200°C. Using a hammer and the tip of a sturdy knife, poke out the "eyes" in the top of a fresh coconut and pour the liquid into a jug. Finely chop the fish and mix with the tomatoes, bell peppers, onion, and chile. Stir in the bread crumbs, coconut liquid, and salt and pepper.

❷ Grease a 1 lb 2-oz/500-g loaf pan and line the base. Add the fish mixture.

❸ Bake the loaf in the preheated oven for 1–1¼ hours, or until set.

❹ To make the hot pepper sauce, mix the tomato ketchup, hot pepper sauce, and mustard together in a bowl until smooth and creamy.

❺ Cut the loaf into slices and garnish with lemon twists and chervil. Serve hot or cold with the sauce.

Nutritional Information

Calories	138	Sugars	12g
Protein	11g	Fat	1g
Carbohydrate	23g	Saturates	0g

Main Courses

& Side Dishes

Thai Red Chicken

This is a really colorful dish, the red of the tomatoes perfectly complementing the orange of the sweet potato.

serves 4

1 tbsp corn oil	4 lime leaves
1 lb/450 g lean boneless, skinless chicken	8 oz/225 g sweet potato
2 garlic cloves, crushed	2½ cups coconut milk
2 tbsp Thai red curry paste	8 oz/225 g cherry tomatoes, halved
2 tbsp freshly grated galangal	3 tbsp chopped fresh cilantro
or gingerroot	freshly cooked jasmine or Thai fragrant
1 tbsp tamarind paste	rice, to serve

Method

❶ Heat the oil in a preheated wok or large, heavy-bottom pan.

❷ Thinly slice the chicken. Add the chicken to the wok and stir-fry for 5 minutes.

❸ Add the garlic, curry paste, galangal, tamarind paste, and lime leaves to the wok and stir-fry for 1 minute.

❹ Using a sharp knife, peel and dice the sweet potato. Add the coconut milk and sweet potato to the mixture in the wok and bring to a boil. Let bubble over medium heat for 20 minutes, or until the juices begin to thicken and reduce.

❺ Add the cherry tomatoes and chopped cilantro to the curry and cook for an additional 5 minutes, stirring occasionally. Transfer to serving plates and serve hot with freshly cooked rice.

Nutritional Information

Calories	249	Sugars	14g
Protein	26g	Fat	7g
Carbohydrate	22g	Saturates	2g

Jerk Chicken

This is perhaps one of the best known Caribbean dishes. The "jerk" in the name refers to the hot spicy coating.

serves 4

4 lean chicken portions	½ tsp paprika
1 bunch scallions	¼ tsp ground allspice
1–2 fresh Scotch bonnet chiles, seeded	pinch of ground cinnamon
1 garlic clove	pinch of ground cloves
2-inch/5-cm piece fresh gingerroot, coarsely chopped	4 tbsp white wine vinegar
	3 tbsp light soy sauce
½ tsp dried thyme	pepper

Method

❶ Place the chicken portions in a shallow, nonmetallic dish.

❷ Place the scallions, chiles, garlic, ginger, thyme, paprika, allspice, cinnamon, cloves, wine vinegar, soy sauce, and pepper to taste in a food processor and process until smooth.

❸ Pour the spicy mixture over the chicken. Turn the chicken portions over so that they are well coated in the marinade.

❹ Transfer the chicken portions to the refrigerator and let marinate for up to 24 hours.

❺ Preheat the grill. Remove the chicken from the marinade and grill over medium-hot coals for 30 minutes, turning the chicken over and basting occasionally with the marinade, until the chicken is browned and cooked through.

❻ Transfer the chicken portions to individual serving plates and serve.

Nutritional Information

Calories	158	Sugars	0.4g
Protein	29g	Fat	4g
Carbohydrate	2g	Saturates	1g

Ginger Chicken & Corn

Chicken wings and corn in a sticky ginger marinade are designed to be eaten with the fingers—there's no other way!

serves 4

3 fresh corn cobs	**To serve**
12 chicken wings	baked potatoes in their skins
1-inch/2.5-cm piece fresh gingerroot	mixed salad greens
6 tbsp lemon juice	
4 tsp corn oil	
1 tbsp golden superfine sugar	

Method

❶ Preheat the broiler to medium. Remove the husks and silken hairs from the corn cobs. Using a sharp knife, cut each cob into 6 slices. Place in a large bowl with the chicken wings.

❷ Peel the piece of gingerroot and grate or chop finely.

❸ Mix the ginger, lemon juice, corn oil, and sugar together in a bowl, then pour over the corn and chicken and toss until evenly coated.

❹ Thread the corn and chicken wings onto 6 metal skewers, to make turning them easier.

❺ Cook the corn and chicken skewers under the hot broiler, basting with the gingery glaze and turning frequently for 15–20 minutes, or until the corn is golden brown and tender and the chicken is cooked through. Alternatively, cook the skewers on a grill over hot coals. Serve with baked potatoes in their skins and a salad.

Nutritional Information

Calories 123	Sugars 3g
Protein 14g	Fat 6g
Carbohydrate 3g	Saturates 1g

Skewered Spicy Tomato Chicken

These lowfat, spicy skewers are cooked in a matter of minutes. They can be assembled ahead of time and stored in the refrigerator until you need them.

serves 4

1 lb 2 oz/500 g skinless, boneless chicken breasts	1 tbsp chopped fresh rosemary
3 tbsp tomato paste	9 oz/250 g cherry tomatoes
2 tbsp Worcestershire sauce	freshly cooked couscous or rice, to serve
2 tbsp clear honey	fresh rosemary sprigs, to garnish

Method

❶ Preheat the broiler to medium. Using a sharp knife, cut the chicken into 1-inch/2.5-cm chunks and place in a bowl.

❷ Mix the tomato paste, Worcestershire sauce, honey, and chopped rosemary together in a separate bowl. Add to the chicken, stirring to coat evenly.

❸ Thread the chicken pieces and cherry tomatoes alternately onto 8 presoaked wooden skewers, then spoon over any remaining glaze.

❹ Cook the skewers under the hot broiler for 8–10 minutes, turning occasionally, until the chicken is cooked through. Serve immediately on a bed of couscous, garnished with rosemary sprigs.

Nutritional Information

Calories	195	Sugars	11g
Protein	28g	Fat	4g
Carbohydrate	12g	Saturates	1g

Teppanyaki

This simple, Japanese style of cooking is ideal for thinly sliced breast of chicken. Mirin is a rich, sweet rice wine, which is available from Asian food stores.

serves 4

4 boneless chicken breasts	⅔ cup bean sprouts
1 red bell pepper	1 tbsp corn oil
1 green bell pepper	4 tbsp soy sauce
4 scallions	4 tbsp mirin
8 baby corn cobs	1 tbsp grated fresh gingerroot

Method

❶ Using a sharp knife, remove the skin from the chicken and slice at a slight angle, to a thickness of about ¼ inch/ 5 mm.

❷ Seed and thinly slice the bell peppers and slice the scallions and baby corn cobs. Arrange the bell peppers, scallions, baby corn cobs, and bean sprouts on a plate with the sliced chicken.

❸ Heat a large grill pan or heavy-bottom skillet, then lightly brush with oil. Add the vegetables and chicken slices in small batches, leaving space between them so that they cook thoroughly.

❹ Mix the soy sauce, mirin, and ginger together in a small bowl and serve as a dip with the chicken and vegetables.

Variation

If you cannot find mirin, add 1 tablespoon of soft brown sugar to the sauce instead. Instead of serving the sauce as a dip, you could use it as a marinade. However, do not let it marinate for more than 2 hours, otherwise the soy sauce will cause the chicken to dry out and become tough. Use other vegetables, such as snow peas or thinly sliced carrots, if you prefer.

Nutritional Information

Calories	206	Sugars	4g
Protein	30g	Fat	7g
Carbohydrate	6g	Saturates	2g

Beef Teriyaki

This Japanese-style teriyaki sauce complements grilled beef, but it can also be used to accompany chicken or salmon.

serves 4

1 lb/450 g extra thin lean beef steaks

8 scallions, cut into short lengths

1 yellow bell pepper, seeded and
cut into chunks

green salad, to serve

Sauce

1 tsp cornstarch

2 tbsp dry sherry

2 tbsp white wine vinegar

3 tbsp soy sauce

1 tbsp dark muscovado sugar

1 garlic clove, crushed

½ tsp ground cinnamon

½ tsp ground ginger

Method

❶ Place the beef in a shallow, nonmetallic dish. To make the sauce, mix the cornstarch with the sherry until smooth. Place the vinegar, soy sauce, sugar, garlic, cinnamon, and ginger in a bowl and stir in the cornstarch paste. Pour over the beef, then turn to coat and chill for 2 hours.

❷ Preheat the grill. Remove the beef from the sauce, draining well. Pour the sauce into a pan.

❸ Cut the beef into thin strips and thread these, concertina-style, onto several presoaked wooden skewers, alternating each strip of beef with pieces of scallion and yellow bell pepper.

❹ Gently heat the sauce until it is just simmering, stirring occasionally. Grill the kabobs over hot coals for 5–8 minutes, turning and basting the beef and vegetables occasionally with the reserved teriyaki sauce.

❺ Arrange the skewers on serving plates and pour the remaining sauce over the kabobs. Serve immediately with salad.

Nutritional Information

Calories 184		Sugars 6g	
Protein. 24g		Fat. 5g	
Carbohydrate 8g		Saturates. 2g	

Wine-Marinated Steaks

Fillet, sirloin, rump, and entrecôte are all suitable cuts of steak for this dish, although rump steak retains the most flavor.

serves 4

4 rump steaks, about 9 oz/250 g each

4 large portobello mushrooms

olive oil, for brushing

branch of fresh rosemary (optional)

Marinade

2½ cups red wine

1 onion, cut into fourths

2 tbsp Dijon mustard

2 garlic cloves, crushed

salt and pepper

Method

❶ Snip through the fat strip on the steaks in 3 places, so that the steak retains its shape when cooked.

❷ Mix the red wine, onion, mustard, garlic, and salt and pepper together in a bowl. Lay the steaks in a shallow, nonmetallic dish and pour over the marinade. Cover and let chill for 2–3 hours. Remove the steaks from the refrigerator 30 minutes before cooking, to let them come to room temperature.

❸ Preheat the grill. Cook the steaks over hot coals for 1 minute on each side. If the steaks are 1 inch/2.5 cm thick, keep them over the hot grill and cook for 4 minutes on each side for medium-rare steaks, or to taste. If the steaks are thicker, move them farther away from the coals. To test the readiness of the steaks while cooking, press them with your finger—the more the steak yields, the less it is cooked.

❹ Brush the mushrooms with oil. Cook them alongside the steaks for 5 minutes, turning once. Meanwhile, place the rosemary, if using, in the fire to flavor the steaks.

❺ Remove the steaks from the grill and let rest for 1–2 minutes. Slice the mushrooms and serve immediately with the steaks.

Nutritional Information

Calories	356	Sugars	2g
Protein	41g	Fat	9g
Carbohydrate	2g	Saturates	4g

Pork Stroganoff

Tender, lean pork is cooked in a tasty, rich tomato sauce and flavored with a tangy plain yogurt.

serves 4

1 tbsp vegetable oil

12 oz/350 g lean pork fillet, cut into ½-inch/1-cm thick slices

1 onion, chopped

2 garlic cloves, crushed

2 tbsp all-purpose flour

2 tbsp tomato paste

generous 1¾ cups chicken or vegetable stock

generous 2 cups sliced white mushrooms

1 large green bell pepper, halved, seeded, and diced

½ tsp ground nutmeg

salt and pepper

4 tbsp lowfat natural yogurt, plus extra to serve

freshly cooked rice, to serve

To garnish

chopped fresh parsley

ground nutmeg

Method

❶ Heat the oil in a large, heavy-bottom pan. Add the pork, onion, and garlic and gently cook for 4–5 minutes, or until they are lightly browned.

❷ Add the flour and tomato paste, then pour in the stock and stir until mixed thoroughly.

❸ Add the mushrooms, green bell pepper, and nutmeg. Season to taste and bring to a boil. Reduce the heat, then cover and let simmer for 20 minutes, or until the pork is tender and cooked through.

❹ Remove the pan from the heat and stir in the yogurt.

❺ Serve the pork and sauce on a bed of rice, sprinkled with chopped parsley, with an extra spoonful of yogurt and a light dusting of ground nutmeg.

Nutritional Information

Calories 223

Protein. 22g

Carbohydrate 12g

Sugars 7g

Fat. 10g

Saturates 3g

Tangy Pork Fillet

These tasty pork fillets are served with a delicious tangy orange sauce.

serves 4

14 oz/400 g lean pork fillet

salt and pepper

3 tbsp orange marmalade

grated rind and juice of 1 orange

1 tbsp white wine vinegar

dash of Tabasco sauce

Sauce

1 tbsp olive oil

1 small onion, chopped

1 small green bell pepper, halved, seeded,

and thinly sliced

1 tbsp cornstarch

²/₃ cup orange juice

To serve

freshly cooked rice

mixed salad greens

Method

❶ Preheat the grill. Place a large piece of double-thickness foil in a shallow dish. Place the pork in the center of the foil and season with salt and pepper.

❷ Heat the marmalade, orange rind and juice, vinegar, and Tabasco together, stirring until the marmalade melts. Pour over the pork and wrap securely in the foil. Cook over hot coals for 25 minutes, turning occasionally.

❸ To make the sauce, heat the oil in a heavy-bottom pan. Add the onion and cook for 2–3 minutes. Add the green bell pepper and cook for 3–4 minutes.

❹ Remove the pork from the foil and place on the rack. Pour the juices from the pork into the pan with the sauce. Grill the pork for 10–20 minutes, turning, until cooked through.

❺ Mix the cornstarch and orange juice together until smooth. Add to the sauce and cook, stirring, until the sauce has thickened. Slice the pork and spoon the sauce over. Serve with rice and salad.

Nutritional Information

Calories 230
Protein 19g
Carbohydrate 20g
Sugars 16g
Fat 9g
Saturates 3g

Savory Hotchpotch

This hearty lamb stew is full of vegetables and herbs, and is topped with a layer of crisp, golden potato slices—a satisfying family meal.

serves 4

8 middle neck lean lamb chops, neck of lamb, or any lean stewing lamb

salt and pepper

1–2 garlic cloves, crushed

2 lamb's kidneys (optional)

1 large onion, thinly sliced

1 leek, sliced

2–3 carrots, sliced

1 tsp chopped fresh tarragon or sage, or ½ tsp dried tarragon or sage

2 lb 4 oz/1 kg potatoes, thinly sliced

1¼ cups stock

2 tbsp margarine, melted, plus extra for greasing, or 1 tbsp vegetable oil

chopped fresh parsley, to garnish

Method

❶ Preheat the oven to 350°F/180°C. Trim any excess fat from the lamb and season well with salt and pepper. Arrange in a large, ovenproof casserole and sprinkle with the garlic.

❷ If using kidneys, remove the skin. Halve, then cut out the cores. Chop into small pieces and sprinkle them over the lamb.

❸ Place the vegetables over the lamb, letting the pieces slip in between the meat, then sprinkle with the herbs. Arrange the potato on top of the meat and vegetables, in an overlapping pattern.

❹ Bring the stock to a boil and season to taste with salt and pepper, then pour over the casserole. Brush the potatoes with the melted margarine, then cover with greased foil or a lid and cook in the preheated oven for 1½ hours.

❺ Remove the foil from the casserole, increase the temperature to 425°F/220°C and return the casserole to the oven for 30 minutes, or until the potatoes are browned.

❻ Garnish the hotchpotch with chopped parsley and serve immediately.

Nutritional Information

Calories	365	Sugars	5g
Protein	23g	Fat	11g
Carbohydrate	48g	Saturates	4g

Baked Sea Bass

Sea bass is often paired with subtle Asian flavors. Serve the fish with pickled sushi ginger and soy sauce, if liked.

serves 4

corn oil, for brushing (optional)

2 sea bass, about 2 lb 4 oz/1 kg each, gutted and scaled

2 scallions, green part only, cut into strips

2-inch/5-cm piece fresh gingerroot, cut into strips

2 garlic cloves, unpeeled, lightly crushed

2 tbsp mirin or dry sherry

salt and pepper

To serve

pickled sushi ginger (optional)

soy sauce

Method

❶ Preheat the grill. Lay out a double thickness of foil and oil the top piece or lay a piece of parchment paper over the foil.

❷ Place the fish in the middle of the foil and open the cavities. Push a mixture of scallion, ginger, and garlic into each of the cavities.

❸ Pour the mirin over the fish and season to taste with salt and pepper.

❹ Close the cavities and lay each fish on its side. Fold over the foil to encase the fish and seal the edges securely. Fold each end neatly.

❺ Cook over medium–hot coals for 15 minutes, turning once.

❻ To serve, remove the foil and cut each fish into 2–3 pieces. Serve with the pickled sushi ginger, if using, and soy sauce.

Nutritional Information

Calories	140	Sugars	0.1g
Protein	29g	Fat	1g
Carbohydrate	0.1g	Saturates	0.2g

Lemony Angler Fish Skewers

A simple basting sauce is brushed over these tasty kabobs. When served with crusty bread and a green salad, they make a perfect light meal.

serves 4

1 lb/450 g angler fish tail, cut into
2-inch/5-cm chunks

2 zucchini, thickly sliced

1 lemon, cut into wedges

12 cherry tomatoes

8 bay leaves

Sauce

3 tbsp olive oil

2 tbsp lemon juice

1 tsp chopped fresh thyme

½ tsp lemon pepper

salt

To serve

salad greens

fresh crusty bread

Method

❶ Preheat the grill. Thread the angler fish, zucchini, lemon, tomatoes, and bay leaves alternately onto 4 metal skewers.

❷ To make the basting sauce, mix the oil, lemon juice, thyme, lemon pepper, and salt to taste together in a small bowl. Brush the sauce liberally over the kabobs.

❸ Cook the kabobs over medium–hot coals for 15 minutes, basting them frequently with the sauce, until the fish is cooked through. Transfer the skewers to individual serving plates and serve with salad greens and crusty bread.

Nutritional Information

Calories	191	Sugars	2g
Protein	21g	Fat	11g
Carbohydrate	1g	Saturates	1g

Charred Tuna Steaks

Tuna has a firm flesh, which is ideal for grilling, but it can be a little dry unless marinated first.

serves 4

4 tuna steaks

3 tbsp light soy sauce

1 tbsp Worcestershire sauce

1 tsp whole-grain mustard

1 tsp superfine sugar

1 tbsp corn oil

green salad, to serve

To garnish

fresh flatleaf parsley sprigs

lemon wedges

Method

❶ Arrange the tuna steaks in a single layer in a shallow dish.

❷ Mix the soy sauce, Worcestershire sauce, mustard, sugar, and oil together in a small bowl. Pour the marinade over the tuna steaks and gently turn them to coat well.

❸ Cover and let marinate in the refrigerator for at least 30 minutes, or up to 2 hours.

❹ Preheat the grill. Remove the tuna steaks from the marinade, reserving it for basting. Cook over hot coals for 10–15 minutes, turning once and basting frequently with the reserved marinade.

❺ Transfer the tuna steaks to warmed serving plates. Garnish with flatleaf parsley and lemon wedges and serve immediately with a green salad.

Cook's tip

If a marinade contains soy sauce, the marinating time should be limited, usually to 2 hours to prevent the fish from drying out.

Nutritional Information

Calories	153	Sugars	1g
Protein	29g	Fat	3g
Carbohydrate	1g	Saturates	1g

Seafood Stir-Fry

This combination of assorted seafood and tender vegetables flavored
with ginger makes an ideal light meal served with egg noodles.

serves 4

3½ oz/100 g small, thin asparagus spears

1 tbsp corn oil

1-inch/2.5-cm piece fresh gingerroot,
cut into thin strips

1 leek, shredded

2 carrots, cut into very thin strips

3½ oz/100 g baby corn cobs, cut into
fourths lengthwise

2 tbsp light soy sauce

1 tbsp oyster sauce

1 tsp clear honey

1 lb/450 g cooked assorted shellfish,
thawed if frozen

freshly cooked egg noodles, to serve

To garnish

4 cooked large shrimp

small bunch snipped fresh chives

Method

❶ Bring a small pan of water to a
boil. Add the asparagus and blanch for
1–2 minutes. Drain the asparagus and
keep warm.

❷ Heat the oil in a preheated wok or large
skillet. Add the ginger, leek, carrots, and
corn cobs and cook for 3 minutes. Do not
let the vegetables brown.

❸ Add the soy sauce, oyster sauce, and
honey to the wok.

❹ Add the cooked shellfish and continue
to cook, stirring, for 2–3 minutes, or until
the vegetables are just tender and the
shellfish are thoroughly heated through.
Add the blanched asparagus and cook for
2 minutes.

❺ To serve, pile the cooked noodles onto
4 warmed serving plates and spoon the
seafood stir-fry over them. Garnish with
the cooked large shrimp and snipped
chives and serve immediately.

Nutritional Information

Calories	226	Sugars	5g
Protein	35g	Fat	7g
Carbohydrate	6g	Saturates	1g

Biryani with Onions

An assortment of vegetables is cooked here with tender rice, flavored and colored with bright yellow turmeric and other warming Indian spices.

serves 4

scant 1 cup basmati rice, rinsed

scant ¼ cup red lentils, rinsed

1 bay leaf

6 cardamom pods, split

1 tsp ground turmeric

6 whole cloves

1 tsp cumin seeds

1 cinnamon stick, broken

1 onion, chopped

8 oz/225 g cauliflower florets

1 large carrot, diced

scant 1 cup frozen peas

⅓ cup golden raisins

salt and pepper

2½ cups vegetable stock

naan bread, to serve

Caramelized onions

2 tsp vegetable oil

1 red onion, shredded

1 onion, shredded

2 tsp superfine sugar

Method

❶ Place the rice, lentils, bay leaf, spices, onion, cauliflower, carrot, peas, and golden raisins in a large pan. Season to taste with salt and pepper and mix well.

❷ Pour in the stock and bring to a boil. Reduce the heat, then cover and simmer for 15 minutes, stirring occasionally, until the rice is tender. Remove the pan from the heat and leave, covered, for 10 minutes. Discard the bay leaf, cardamoms, cloves, and cinnamon stick.

❸ To make the caramelized onions, heat the oil in a skillet. Add the onions and cook them over medium heat for 3–4 minutes, or until softened. Add the sugar, increase the heat, and cook, stirring constantly, for an additional 2–3 minutes, or until the onions are golden.

❹ Gently mix the rice and vegetables together and transfer to warmed serving plates. Spoon over the onions and serve immediately with naan bread.

Nutritional Information

Calories	223	Sugars	18g
Protein	8g	Fat	4g
Carbohydrate	42g	Saturates	1g

Moroccan Salad

Couscous is a type of semolina made from durum wheat. It is wonderful in salads, because it readily absorbs the flavor of the dressing.

serves 4

1 cup couscous

1 bunch scallions, finely chopped

1 small green bell pepper, halved, seeded, and chopped

4-inch/10-cm piece cucumber, chopped

6 oz/175 g canned chickpeas, drained and rinsed

⅓ cup raisins or golden raisins

salt and pepper

few lettuce leaves

2 oranges, peeled and segmented

fresh mint sprigs, to garnish

Dressing

rind of 1 orange, finely grated

1 tbsp chopped fresh mint

⅔ cup plain yogurt

Method

❶ Place the couscous in a bowl and pour over enough boiling water to cover. Let soak for 15 minutes or until the grains are tender, then stir gently with a fork to separate them.

❷ Add the scallions, green bell pepper, cucumber, chickpeas, and golden raisins to the couscous, stirring well. Season to taste with salt and pepper.

❸ To make the dressing, place the orange rind, mint, and yogurt in a small bowl and mix together until well blended. Pour the dressing over the couscous mixture and stir to mix well.

❹ Arrange the lettuce leaves on 4 serving plates. Divide the couscous mixture between the plates and arrange the orange segments on top. Garnish with fresh mint sprigs and serve.

Nutritional Information

Calories	195	Sugars	15g
Protein	8g	Fat	2g
Carbohydrate	40g	Saturates	0.3g

Mushroom Cannelloni

Thick pasta tubes are filled with a mixture of seasoned chopped mushrooms and baked in a rich, fragrant tomato sauce.

serves 4

12 oz/350 g cremini mushrooms, finely chopped

1 onion, finely chopped

1 garlic clove, crushed

1 tbsp chopped fresh thyme

½ tsp freshly grated nutmeg

4 tbsp dry white wine

scant 1 cup fresh white bread crumbs

salt and pepper

12 dried "quick-cook" cannelloni tubes

shavings of fresh Parmesan cheese, to garnish (optional)

Tomato sauce

1 red bell pepper, halved, and seeded

generous ¾ cup dry white wine

1¾ cups strained tomatoes

2 tbsp tomato paste

2 bay leaves

1 tsp superfine sugar

Method

❶ Preheat the oven to 400°F/200°C and preheat the broiler. Place the mushrooms, onion, and garlic in a pan. Stir in the thyme, nutmeg, and wine. Bring to a boil, then cover and simmer for 10 minutes. Stir in the bread crumbs and season to taste. Cool for 10 minutes.

❷ To make the sauce, place the bell pepper on a broiler rack and cook under the hot broiler for 8–10 minutes, until charred. Cool, then peel off the skin. Chop the flesh and place in a food processor with the wine. Blend until smooth, then pour into a pan. Add the remaining sauce ingredients and mix. Bring to a boil and simmer for 10 minutes. Discard the bay leaves.

❸ Cover the base of a large, ovenproof dish with a thin layer of sauce. Fill the cannelloni with the mushroom mixture and place in a single layer in the dish. Spoon over the remaining sauce, then cover and bake in the oven for 35–40 minutes. Garnish with Parmesan cheese shavings, if using, and serve.

Nutritional Information

Calories	156	Sugars	8g
Protein	6g	Fat	1g
Carbohydrate	21g	Saturates	0.2g

Desserts

Spun Sugar Pears

Whole pears are poached in a Madeira syrup in the microwave, then served with
a delicate spun sugar surround.

serves 4

²/₃ cup water

²/₃ cup sweet Madeira wine

generous ¹/₂ cup superfine sugar

2 tbsp lime juice

4 ripe pears, peeled, stems left on

fresh mint sprigs, to decorate

Spun sugar

generous ¹/₂ cup superfine sugar

3 tbsp water

Method

❶ Blend the water, Madeira, sugar, and lime juice together in a large bowl. Cover and cook on High power for 3 minutes. Stir well until the sugar dissolves.

❷ Cut a thin slice from the base of each pear, so that they stand upright. Add the pears to the bowl, spooning the wine syrup over them. Cover and cook on High power for 10 minutes, until they are tender. Let cool, covered, in the syrup.

❸ Remove the pears from the syrup and let stand on serving plates. Cook the syrup, uncovered, on High power for 15 minutes, or until reduced by half and thickened slightly. Let stand for 5 minutes, then spoon the syrup over the pears.

❹ To make the spun sugar, mix the sugar and water together in a bowl. Cook, uncovered, on High power for 1¹/₂ minutes. Stir until the sugar has dissolved completely. Continue to cook on High power for a further 5–6 minutes, or until the sugar has caramelized.

❺ Wait for the caramel bubbles to subside and leave to stand for 2 minutes. Dip a teaspoon in the caramel and spin sugar around each pear in a circular motion. Decorate with mint sprigs and serve.

Nutritional Information

Calories	166	Sugars	41g
Protein	0.3g	Fat	0g
Carbohydrate	41g	Saturates	0g

Summer Fruit Clafoutis

Serve this mouthwatering French-style, fruit-in-batter dessert hot or cold with lowfat ricotta or yogurt.

serves 4

1 lb 2 oz/500 g prepared fresh assorted soft fruits, such as blackberries, raspberries, strawberries, blueberries, gooseberries, red currants, and black currants

4 tbsp soft fruit liqueur, such as kirsch, crème de cassis, or framboise

4 tbsp skim milk powder

generous ⅔ cup all-purpose flour

pinch of salt

generous ¼ cup superfine sugar

2 eggs, beaten

1¼ cups skim milk

1 tsp vanilla extract

2 tsp superfine sugar, for dusting

To serve

assorted soft fruits

lowfat yogurt or ricotta

Method

❶ Place the assorted soft fruits in a large bowl and spoon over the fruit liqueur. Cover and let chill for 1 hour for the fruit to macerate.

❷ Mix the skim milk powder, flour, salt, and sugar together in a bowl. Make a well in the center and, using a balloon whisk, gradually whisk in the eggs, milk, and vanilla extract until smooth. Transfer to a pitcher and reserve for 30 minutes.

❸ Preheat the oven to 400°F/200°C. Line the base of a 9-inch/23-cm round ovenproof dish with parchment paper, and spoon in the fruits and juices.

❹ Whisk the batter again and pour it over the fruits. Stand the dish on a baking sheet and bake in the preheated oven for 50 minutes, or until firm, risen, and golden brown.

❺ Dust with superfine sugar. Serve immediately with extra fruits and yogurt.

Nutritional Information

Calories	228	Sugars	26g
Protein	9g	Fat	2g
Carbohydrate	42g	Saturates	1g

Summer Fruit Salad

A mixture of soft summer fruits in an orange-flavored syrup with a dash of port, served with lowfat ricotta.

serves 6

scant ½ cup superfine sugar

5 tbsp water

grated rind and juice of 1 small orange

generous 1 cup red currants, stripped from their stems

2 tsp arrowroot

2 tbsp port

½ cup blackberries

½ cup blueberries

generous ¾ cup strawberries

1¼ cups raspberries

lowfat ricotta, to serve

Method

❶ Place the sugar, water, and grated orange rind in a heavy-bottom pan and heat gently, stirring until the sugar has dissolved.

❷ Add the red currants and orange juice, then bring to a boil and simmer gently for 2–3 minutes.

❸ Strain the fruit, reserving the syrup, and place in a bowl.

❹ Blend the arrowroot with a little water. Return the syrup to the pan, then add the arrowroot and bring to a boil, stirring constantly until thickened.

❺ Add the port and mix well. Pour the syrup over the red currants in the bowl.

❻ Add the blackberries, blueberries, strawberries, and raspberries to the bowl. Mix the fruit together and let cool until required.

❼ Serve in individual glass dishes with ricotta.

Nutritional Information

Calories	110	Sugars	26g
Protein	1g	Fat	0.1g
Carbohydrate	26g	Saturates	0g

Fruity Muffins

Perfect for those on a lowfat diet and for weight watchers, these little cakes contain no butter, just a little corn oil.

makes 10

2 cups whole-wheat self-rising flour

2 tsp baking powder

2 heaping tbsp muscovado sugar

generous ½ cup ready-to-eat
dried apricots, finely chopped

1 banana, mashed with 1 tbsp orange juice

1 tsp finely grated orange rind

1¼ cups skim milk

1 egg, beaten

3 tbsp corn oil

2 tbsp porridge oats

fruit spread, honey, or maple syrup,
to serve

Method

❶ Preheat the oven to 400°F/200°C. Place 10 paper muffin cases in a deep patty tin. Sift the flour and baking powder into a large bowl, adding any bran that remains in the sifter. Stir in the sugar and apricots.

❷ Make a well in the center of the dry ingredients and add the mashed banana, orange rind, milk, beaten egg, and oil. Mix together to form a thick batter.

❸ Divide the batter evenly between the 10 paper cases. Sprinkle the tops with a few porridge oats and bake in the preheated oven for 25–30 minutes, or until well risen and firm to the touch, or until a skewer inserted into the center comes out clean. Transfer the muffins to a wire rack to cool slightly. Serve the muffins while they are warm with a little fruit spread.

Nutritional Information

Calories	162	Sugars	11g
Protein	4g	Fat	4g
Carbohydrate	28g	Saturates	1g

Strawberry Meringues

The combination of aromatic strawberries and rosewater with crisp caramelized sugar meringues makes this a truly irresistible dessert.

serves 4

3 egg whites

pinch of salt

generous 1 cup light muscovado sugar, crushed

1½ cups strawberries, hulled

2 tsp rose water

⅔ cup lowfat ricotta

extra strawberries, to serve (optional)

To decorate

rose petals

rose-scented geranium leaves

Method

❶ Preheat the oven to 250°F/120°C. Whisk the egg whites and salt together in a clean bowl until very stiff and dry. Gradually whisk in the sugar, a spoonful at a time, until stiff again.

❷ Line a baking sheet with parchment paper and drop 12 spoonfuls of the meringue mixture onto it. Bake in the preheated oven for 3–3½ hours, or until completely dried out and crisp. Let cool.

❸ Reserve ⅓ cup of the strawberries. Place the remaining strawberries in a food processor or blender and process for a few seconds until smooth.

❹ Alternatively, mash the strawberries with a fork and press through a strainer to form a purée. Stir in the rose water. Let chill until required.

❺ To serve, slice the reserved strawberries lengthwise. Sandwich the meringues together with ricotta and sliced strawberries.

❻ Spoon the strawberry rose purée onto 6 serving plates and top with a meringue. Decorate with rose petals and rose-scented geranium leaves, and serve with extra strawberries, if using.

Nutritional Information

Calories	145	Sugars	35g
Protein	3g	Fat	0.3g
Carbohydrate	35g	Saturates	0.1g

Almond Trifles

These trifles can be made with any type of fruit, even frozen. When they thaw, the juices will soak into the cookie base—delicious!

serves 4

8 amaretti cookies, crushed	1¼ cups lowfat ricotta
4 tbsp brandy or Amaretto liqueur	2 heaping tbsp toasted slivered almonds
1¼ cups raspberries	1 tsp unsweetened cocoa
1¼ cups canned lowfat custard	
1 tsp almond extract	

Method

❶ Divide the amaretti cookies between 4 dessert glasses. Sprinkle over the brandy and let stand for 30 minutes, or until softened.

❷ Top the cookies with a layer of raspberries, reserving a few for decoration, and spoon over enough custard just to cover.

❸ Mix the almond extract and ricotta together and spoon the mixture over the custard, smoothing the surface. Let chill in the refrigerator for 30 minutes.

❹ Before serving, sprinkle with toasted almonds and dust with unsweetened cocoa.

❺ Decorate the trifles with the reserved raspberries and serve immediately.

Nutritional Information

Calories	241	Sugars	23g
Protein	9g	Fat	6g
Carbohydrate	35g	Saturates	2g

Mixed Fruit Brûlées

Traditionally a rich mixture made with cream, this fruit-based version is just as tempting using lowfat sour cream and ricotta as a topping.

serves 4

1 lb/450 g prepared assorted summer
fruits, such as strawberries, raspberries,
black currants, red currants, and cherries,
thawed if frozen

²/₃ cup sour cream

²/₃ cup lowfat ricotta

1 tsp vanilla extract

4 tbsp raw sugar

Method

❶ Preheat the broiler. Divide the prepared strawberries, raspberries, black currants, red currants, and cherries evenly between 4 small heatproof ramekin dishes.

❷ Mix the sour cream, ricotta, and vanilla extract together, then spoon over the fruit, to cover it completely.

❸ Top each serving with 1 tablespoon of raw sugar and place the desserts under the hot broiler for 2–3 minutes, or until the sugar melts completely and begins to caramelize. Let the mixed fruit brûlées stand for 2 minutes before serving.

Cook's tip

Vegetarians should read the labels carefully when buying lowfat products, such as sour cream, because some brands are thickened with nonvegetarian gelatin and other additives.

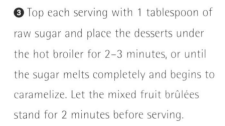

Nutritional Information

Calories	165	Sugars	21g
Protein	5g	Fat	7g
Carbohydrate	21g	Saturates	5g

Paper-Thin Fruit Pies

Perfect for weight watchers, these crisp pastry shells, filled with fruit and glazed with apricot jelly, are best served hot with lowfat custard.

serves 4

1 eating apple	2 tbsp low-sugar apricot jelly
1 ripe pear	1 tbsp unsweetened orange juice
2 tbsp lemon juice	1 tbsp finely chopped pistachios
¼ cup lowfat spread	2 tsp confectioners' sugar, for dusting
8 oz/225 g phyllo pastry, thawed if frozen	lowfat custard, to serve

Method

❶ Preheat the oven to 400°F/200°C. Core and thinly slice the apple and pear and toss them in the lemon juice to prevent them discoloring.

❷ Melt the lowfat spread in a small pan over low heat. Cut the sheets of pastry into 4 and cover with a clean, damp dish towel. Brush 4 nonstick, shallow pans, measuring 4 inches/10 cm across, with a little of the lowfat spread.

❸ Working on each pie separately, brush 4 sheets of pastry with lowfat spread. Press a small sheet of pastry into the base of 1 tin. Arrange the other sheets of pastry on top at slightly different angles. Repeat with the remaining sheets of pastry to make another 3 pies. Arrange the apple and pear slices alternately in the center of each pastry shell and lightly crimp the edges of the pastry of each pie.

❹ Mix the jelly and orange juice together until smooth and brush over the fruit. Bake in the preheated oven for 12–15 minutes. Sprinkle with the pistachios and dust lightly with confectioners' sugar. Serve hot with lowfat custard.

Nutritional Information

Calories	158	Sugars	12g
Protein	2g	Fat	10g
Carbohydrate	14g	Saturates	2g

Mocha Swirl Mousse

A feather-light yet richly moreish combination, these chocolate and coffee mousses are attractive presented in tall glasses.

serves 4

1 tbsp coffee and chicory extract

2 tsp unsweetened cocoa, plus extra for dusting

1 tsp lowfat instant cocoa mix

²/₃ cup lowfat sour cream, plus 4 tsp to serve

2 tsp powdered gelozone

2 tbsp boiling water

2 large egg whites

2 tbsp superfine sugar

4 chocolate coffee beans, to serve

Method

❶ Place the coffee and chicory extract in a bowl, and the unsweetened cocoa and instant cocoa mix in a second bowl. Divide the sour cream between the 2 bowls and mix both well.

❷ Dissolve the gelozone in the boiling water and reserve. Whisk the egg whites and sugar in a clean, greasefree bowl until stiff and divide this evenly between the 2 mixtures.

❸ Divide the dissolved gelozone between the 2 mixtures and, using a large metal spoon, gently fold, until well mixed.

❹ Spoon small amounts of the 2 mousses alternately into 4 serving glasses and swirl together gently. Let chill for 1 hour, or until set.

❺ To serve, top each mousse with a teaspoonful of sour cream, a chocolate coffee bean, and a light dusting of cocoa powder. Serve immediately.

Cook's tip

Gelozone, the vegetarian equivalent of gelatin, is available from most health food stores.

Nutritional Information

Calories	136	Sugars	10g
Protein	5g	Fat	8g
Carbohydrate	11g	Saturates	5g

Orange Syllabub

This is a zesty, creamy whip made from yogurt and milk with a hint of orange, served with light and luscious sweet sponge cakes.

serves 4

4 oranges

2½ cups lowfat plain yogurt

6 tbsp skim milk powder

4 tbsp superfine sugar

1 tbsp grated orange rind

4 tbsp orange juice

2 egg whites

strips of orange zest, to decorate

Sponge hearts

2 eggs

6 tbsp superfine sugar

scant ⅓ cup all-purpose flour

scant ⅓ cup whole-wheat flour

1 tbsp hot water

1 tsp confectioners' sugar

Method

❶ Slice off the tops and bottoms of the oranges and remove the skin. Cut out the segments, removing the zest and the membranes. Divide the segments between 4 dessert glasses, then let chill.

❷ Mix the yogurt, milk powder, sugar, orange rind, and juice together. Cover and chill for 1 hour. Whisk the egg whites until stiff, then fold into the yogurt mixture. Spoon onto the orange slices and chill for 1 hour. Decorate with orange zest.

❸ Preheat the oven to 425°F/220°C. To make the sponge hearts, line a

6 x 10-inch/15 x 25-cm baking pan with parchment paper. Whisk the eggs and superfine sugar together until thick and pale. Sift the flours, then fold into the eggs, adding the hot water at the same time. Pour into the prepared pan and bake in the preheated oven for 9–10 minutes, until golden on top and firm to the touch.

❹ Turn the sponge out onto a sheet of parchment paper. Using a 2-inch/5-cm heart-shaped cutter, stamp out hearts from the sponge. Transfer to a wire rack to cool. Lightly dust with confectioners' sugar before serving with the syllabub.

Nutritional Information

Calories 464

Protein. 22g

Carbohydrate 89g

Sugars 74g

Fat. 5g

Saturates. 2g

Fruit & Nut Loaf

This loaf is like a fruit bread which may be served warm or cold, perhaps spread
with a little margarine or butter or topped with jelly.

serves 4

1½ cups bread flour, plus extra
for dusting

½ tsp salt

1 tbsp margarine, plus extra for greasing

2 tbsp soft light brown sugar

scant ⅓ cup no-soak dried apricots,
chopped

generous ½ cup golden raisins

⅓ cup chopped hazelnuts

2 tsp active dry yeast

6 tbsp orange juice

6 tbsp lowfat plain yogurt

2 tbsp strained apricot jelly

Method

❶ Sift the flour and salt into a large bowl.
Rub in the margarine and stir in the sugar,
apricots, golden raisins, nuts, and yeast.

❷ Warm the orange juice in a pan, but do
not let it boil.

❸ Stir the warm orange juice into the
flour mixture with the yogurt and bring
the mixture together to form a dough.

❹ Knead the dough on a lightly floured
counter for 5 minutes, or until smooth
and elastic. Shape into a circle and place
on a lightly greased baking sheet. Cover
with a clean dish towel and let stand
in a warm place until doubled in size.

❺ Preheat the oven to 425°F/220°C.
Cook the loaf in the preheated oven for
35–40 minutes, or until cooked through.
Transfer to a wire rack and brush the cake
with the apricot jelly. Let the cake cool
before serving.

Nutritional Information

Calories	531	Sugars	53g
Protein	12g	Fat	14g
Carbohydrate	96g	Saturates	2g

Carrot & Ginger Cake

This melt-in-the-mouth version of a favorite cake has a fraction
of the fat of the traditional cake.

serves 10

butter, for greasing

1½ cups all-purpose flour

1 tsp baking soda

1 tsp baking powder

2 tsp ground ginger

½ tsp salt

generous ¾ cup light muscovado sugar

8 oz/225 g carrots, grated

2 pieces preserved ginger, chopped

1 oz/25 g grated fresh gingerroot

⅓ cup seedless raisins

2 eggs, beaten

3 tbsp corn oil

juice of 1 orange

Frosting

1cup lowfat soft cheese

4 tbsp confectioners' sugar

1 tsp vanilla extract

To decorate

grated carrot

finely chopped preserved ginger

ground ginger

Method

❶ Preheat the oven to 350°F/180°C. Grease and line an 8-inch/20-cm round cake pan with parchment paper.

❷ Sift the flour, baking soda, baking powder, ground ginger, and salt into a large bowl. Stir in the sugar, carrots, preserved ginger, gingerroot, and raisins. Beat the eggs, oil, and orange juice together, then pour into the bowl and mix well. Spoon into the pan and bake in the preheated oven for 1–1¼ hours, or until firm to the touch, or a skewer inserted into the center of the cake comes out clean. Let cool completely in the pan.

❸ To make the frosting, beat the cheese until soft. Sift in the sugar and add the vanilla extract. Mix well. Remove the cake from the pan and smooth the frosting over it. Decorate with carrot, preserved ginger, and ground ginger and serve.

Nutritional Information

Calories	249	Sugars	28g
Protein	7g	Fat	6g
Carbohydrate	46g	Saturates	1g

Recipe List

- Almond Trifles *82* • Baked Sea Bass *56* • Beef Teriyaki *46*

- Beef & Vegetable Soup *14* • Biryani with Onions *64* • Bruschetta *24*

- Carrot & Ginger Cake *94* • Charred Tuna Steaks *60* • Cheese & Chive Biscuits *26*

- Chicken & Almond Rissoles *20* • Fruit & Nut Loaf *92* • Fruity Muffins *78*

- Ginger Chicken & Corn *40* • Jerk Chicken *38* • Lemony Angler Fish Skewers *58*

- Lentil & Ham Soup *12* • Minted Onion Bhajis *18* • Mixed Fruit Brûlées *84*

- Mocha Swirl Mousse *88* • Moroccan Salad *66* • Mushroom Cannelloni *68*

- Orange Syllabub *90* • Paper-Thin Fruit Pies *86* • Pork Stroganoff *50*

- Potatoes with a Spicy Filling *28* • Red Snapper & Coconut Loaf *32*

- Rice & Tuna Bell Peppers *30* • Savory Hotchpotch *54* • Seafood Stir-Fry *62*

- Skewered Spicy Tomato Chicken *42* • Spun Sugar Pears *72*

- Strawberry Meringues *80* • Summer Fruit Clafoutis *74* • Summer Fruit Salad *76*

- Sweet & Sour Drumsticks *22* • Tangy Pork Fillet *52* • Teppanyaki *44*

- Thai Red Chicken *36* • Tomato & Red Bell Pepper Soup *10*

- Wine-Marinated Steaks *48* • Yogurt & Spinach Soup *16*